HOW TO: PASS YOUR DRIVING TEST

A SIMPLE GUIDE

BY CRAIG PREEDY DVSA ADI

©Craig Preedy 2020

Craig Preedy DVSA ADI
Herefordshire
www.wyedrive.co.uk

CONTENTS

About the Author

Introduction

1. How to pass your driving test

2. Choosing a Driving Instructor

3. The Theory Test

4. The Practical Test

5. Observation at Junctions

6. Response to Signs – Traffic Lights

7. Use of Mirrors

8. Positioning – Normal Driving

9. Steering Control

10. Safety When Moving Off

11. Turning Right at Junctions

12. Control - When Reverse Parking

13. Control – When Moving Off

14. Response to Signals – Traffic Signs

15. Other Common Pitfalls

16. Managing Test Day Nerves

17. After the Driving Test

    Useful Links

    Your Driving Details

ABOUT THE AUTHOR

Craig has been a qualified driving instructor (DVSA ADI) since 2004 and since 2008 has held the Top Grade awarded to driving instructors. Prior to being an ADI, he worked for various blue chip companies as a training and development manager. When he was made redundant in 2003, he decided to retrain and take those skills of coaching and development into driver training.

Since qualifying as an ADI, Craig has obtained his Fleet Trainer accreditation which has allowed him to work with many companies providing driver coaching for business drivers. He has also passed the Institute of Advanced Motorists Advanced Driving Test and has achieved five gold awards for the RoSPA Advanced Driving Test, considered to be the most advanced test a civilian driver can take.

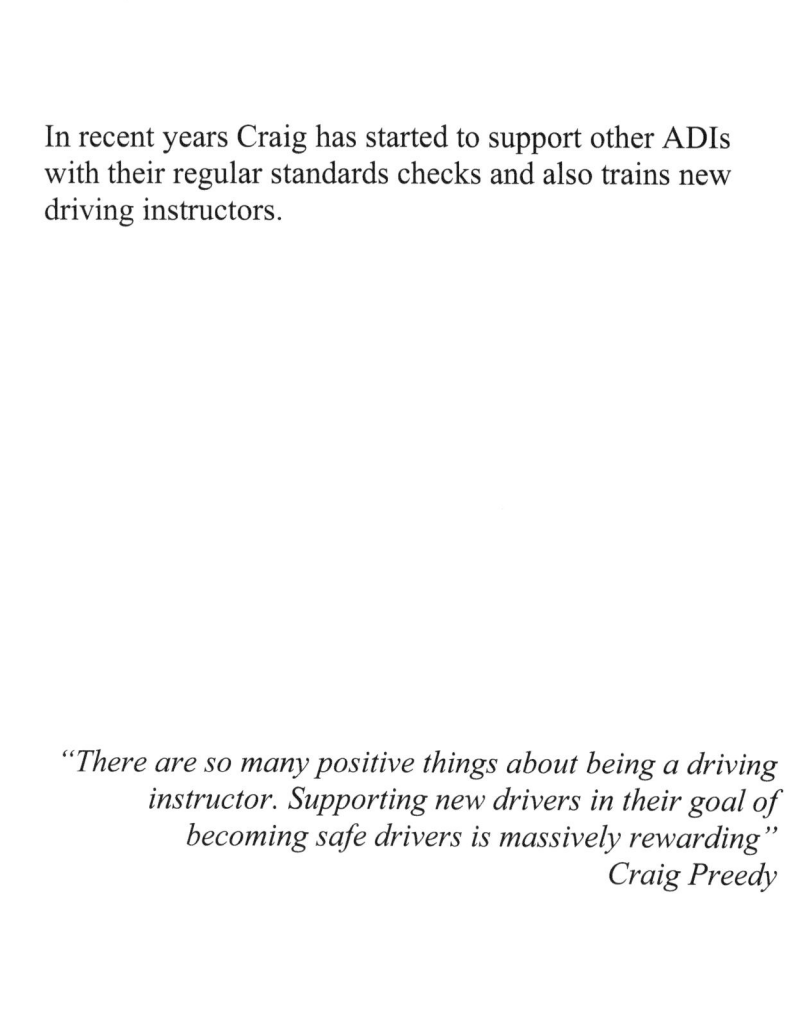

In recent years Craig has started to support other ADIs with their regular standards checks and also trains new driving instructors.

"There are so many positive things about being a driving instructor. Supporting new drivers in their goal of becoming safe drivers is massively rewarding"
Craig Preedy

With thanks and love to my friends Gordon and Val O'Neill without whom my career may have stalled. You were a great influence on my road to becoming a better driving instructor.

Thank you to all of my students for being so brilliant. Not everyone passes first time but each one of you has helped to make me a better instructor.

Thank you to my wife Stella for being so patient with me, especially when I was training to become a driving instructor! I could never have achieved what I have without your support. xx

INTRODUCTION

In this book, I have taken a simple approach looking at what's involved in learning to drive. I will give advice on how to choose a driving instructor and look at the top reasons why people fail their driving tests. I give simple but practical advice on how to avoid the same outcome.

This book can be useful to anyone thinking of learning to drive, who has already started or considering teaching someone such as a family friend or family member.

I will explain the common pitfalls for students taking the theory and practical driving tests. I will look at the most common reasons why people fail and explain ways to overcome them. I'll also give you some practical advice about how to keep calm on test day.

You cannot escape the fact, that in modern society, not many young people have actually failed in anything. I don't mean this to sound derogatory, far from it, but the line of pass and fail in education or sports is not as black and white as it once was. Our school system is designed to see success, which is no bad thing, but sadly when faced with the prospect of actually failing something, it can be the cause of much anxiety.

For some, the driving test might actually be the first occasion where there is a very real possibility of not succeeding at something. Unlike many other tests, there is no grading structure. The end result is simply a pass or a fail.

I hope that by reading through these pages it will help you to understand the most common reasons for failing. Also, to allay some of the fears that you might have when it comes to taking your theory test and practical driving test.

By focusing on the top ten reasons why people fail their test I feel that we are able to look at how some of the practical skills required to overcome failure in these areas can also be applied to all aspects of your driving.

If you have prepared well, there should be no reason why you will not pass the practical driving test, at the first attempt.

Good Luck!

1.
HOW TO PASS YOUR DRIVING TEST

In all my years as a driving instructor, I can count on one hand the number of people who were not nervous before their driving test. Being nervous is a natural way to feel when doing tests of any sort. You may have prepared well and be confident, but you can still feel nervous.

I can recall doing my driving test many years ago and feeling nervous. I was sure I was ready to be on the roads after about eighteen hours of tuition. My driving instructor, Denis, was awesome. Yet, I failed. I cannot remember the exact reason why, other than I think it had something to do with reversing around a corner. A manoeuvre which I hated with a passion.

My second driving test didn't fare much better. I had the same examiner as the first time. I wasn't a fan of his monotone direction but, this time I failed for something different. It was a meeting situation where I braked so hard the examiner ended up on the dashboard. I'm not convinced he had his seat belt on!

On the third attempt I passed. I felt much calmer and thought to myself before the test I either will or I won't. There was no in between. The result would be conclusive one way or another. It was January 17, A few months before my 18th birthday. I had taken another ten hours of lessons between the two previous fails. Surely now I was ready. I don't recall how many faults I had. All I remember is that I passed. It had taken me nine months to pass my test. Some of my friends had passed first time but now it was my turn.

My experience of the driving test all those years ago, is not much different to the experience of learners today. Of course, the test has changed a little since I did mine, but one thing is still true, students do, and will get nervous. I want you to know here and now that there is nothing to be concerned about that good, effective preparation cannot resolve.

Everyone who learns to drive wants and hopes to pass their driving test at the first attempt. The idea of failure is almost unbearable for some. In fact, students often tell me, it's not so much the test that makes them nervous, it's the idea of not passing it! Is that the same for you?

If you are confident in your ability and you focus on driving well, then there should be no reason why failing is even an option.

Please don't mistake confidence for test readiness. I hear of many students who want to book their driving test way before they are ready! Remember, you are paying your driving instructor to prepare you for safe driving, not just for the test. The goal is to be safe for life on all types of road. It is your life and the lives of your fellow road users that should always be a priority. Of course, you might be the most ready and confident person ever to take a test and you could still not pass. Some put this down to bad luck on the day. But, let's think about that. Bad luck on the day? Should you not be ready for as many situations as possible. Later, when you read about the ten most common reasons for failing you will see that none of these are about bad luck on the day. No amount of preparation can expect to cover every likely situation. But, experience on the road will help you to gain more knowledge.

So how do you pass the driving test? Well, quite simply the answer is to think safety at all times. Am I safe? Am I keeping others safe?

Remember, after this 40 minute test you could be driving on the roads, on your own. You are expected to have the skills and knowledge to join your fellow road users and they have an expectation that you will not cause them harm. That is, I think, a very reasonable expectation. Facts are facts though and statistically there is a one in five chance that you will have a crash of some kind within your first six months driving after passing your driving test. How do we define a crash? A crash is quite simply when your vehicle is in collision with another vehicle, road user or object.

To put this into perspective, crashes are caused as follows

- ☐ 1% - Mechanical Failure

- ☐ 4% - Acts of God, such as the driver taking ill at the wheel

- ☐ **95% - Driver Error**

So, there you have it. Almost all crashes involve driver error. You could blame icy conditions, heavy rain or speeding and I agree that these are certainly factors in crashes, but they are not the cause.

When you fail a driving test, it's not someone else's fault! It's certainly not the examiners fault either. **It's your fault**!

There might be factors in the actions of another road user that influenced your decision making but ultimately the decision making is yours and if you are to be independent then you need to take responsibility for your own decisions. Are you ready for that responsibility? Decision making on a driving test does feel strangely different to the decision making you might do when you are driving on your own.

You may have already found that on lessons with your instructor, you behave differently to how you do if driving with a family member. I get told a great deal by parents of how comfortable they feel when they are in the passenger seat and yet when that same student is on their driving lesson, I don't always see the same driver that they see.

I find that on lessons students can try a little too hard to get everything just right. A tendency to overthink every situation for fear of doing the wrong thing. All you need to concern yourself with is are you about to make a safe choice or a reckless choice.

On your lesson, you know your instructor is there and will keep you safe at all times. It's easy to ask them what you should be doing now. When you are first learning this is fine and your instructor expects these types of questions, and they will guide you through various situations but at some point, they will be looking to see your independence. The less they speak, the more independent you are being.

Your role on a driving lessons is to begin to think as a driver and make decisions just as a full licence holder would. Once your driving test is booked, your instructor should be encouraging you to make these decisions. If you're not sure what you should be doing and are tempted to ask your instructor for help, first ask yourself

"What would I do if I was on my own?"

The sooner you start to consider this, the quicker this habit of risk assessment for various situations will develop. That is what you are doing all the time when driving, risk assessing.
This book is called "How to Pass Your Driving Test" and as such you might have been expecting some sort of magic formulae.

You are probably realising that the magic formula for passing your test is not your instructor, a quiet time of day for your test or the right day of the week, or even the examiner with the best local reputation.

The magic formula for a test pass is YOU!

A good instructor will help you get the best out of yourself and be encouraging your development in becoming a safe and confident driver. One who is able to make effective decisions in all types of scenarios.

Choosing the right instructor for you is an important part of the process and in the next chapter I will give you some tips on how to do just that.

2.
CHOOSING A DRIVING INSTRUCTOR

There is no law that states you must use a driving instructor for your driving lessons. If you have access to a vehicle and someone* who is prepared to teach you then there is no reason why you couldn't learn to drive without the need for a qualified driving instructor.

**The rules for supervising a learner driver is that you must be aat least 21 years old. Have a full driving licence (for the type of vehicle they are supervising in — manual or automatic), which must have been held for a minimum of three years. Ensure the car is* *in a safe and legal condition. Meet the minimum eyesight standards.*

If you have not chosen a driving instructor, then it can be a confusing process. There are literally hundreds of driving instructors in each county of the country. Knowing who is the best is difficult. So hopefully this will help you make the right choice.

WHAT EXACTLY IS A DRIVING INSTRUCTOR?

A Driving and Vehicle Standards Agency Approved Driving Instructor (DVSA ADI) is someone who has taken and passed three challenging exams. One theory test and two practical tests. Part One, Part Two and Part Three. Before beginning their training, a potential driving instructor (PDI) must also pass a Disclosure and Barring Service (DBS) check.

Part One of the DVSA ADI exams is the instructor's theory test. This is similar to the learner theory test with the exception of the inclusion of questions relating to teaching new drivers and advanced driving skills.

The PDI will need to score at least 85/100 to pass this part. They can have as many attempts at part one as they need but, once passed, they then have two years to take and pass the part two and part three tests.

Part Two is the PDI's driving test. They have to take and pass a driving test at a higher standard than a learner driver. They get three attempts at this part of the process.

Failure to pass within three attempts means they will need to wait for two years before beginning the process again.

Part Three is the most challenging element of the test. 75% of PDI's don't pass this part of the test. As with Part Two, they have up to three attempts. Failure to pass within three attempts means a two year wait before starting the process again.

A PDI may opt to obtain a trainee licence. This means that they would have completed a minimum 40 hours of training required before taking the Part 3 exam. They will be supervised regularly and will be able to offer tuition for reward. Some schools that use trainee instructors offer cheaper lessons with a trainee. By applying for a trainee licencee it can provide a valuable way for a PDI to gain valuable experience with real students before taking their final exam. You can identify a trainee instructor by their badge. It is a pink triangle.

Once the PDI has passed the final part three of the qualifying tests then they will receive a grade. They will also be invited to apply for their full ADI badge. This is different to the trainee licence as it is green and octagonal in shape. The grade allocated is an indication of their level of ability as an instructor. The grade is either A or B. Only 30% of instructors are a grade A.

Grade A - a minimum score of 43 to 51. This means that the instructor has shown a high standard of instruction

Grade B - 31 to 42. This means that the instructor has shown a satisfactory level of instruction. This is the minimum standard required in order to be called a DVSA ADI. Around 70% of instructors are a Grade B.

To maintain their inclusion on the DVSA register of Approved Driving Instructors, an ADI must take a standards check every two to four years. This can be a stressful time for an ADI. They will need to demonstrate their skills as a driving instructor by delivering a lesson to one of their students whilst a Supervising Examiner observes from the back seat. So, you see, a driving instructor understands what it's like to be on test, and the anxieties associated with it.

RECOMMENDATION

The best way of choosing a driving instructor is generally through recommendation. Who are your family members or friends learning with? It's a good place to start. Driving instructors thrive on their reputation so, recommendation is always a good place to begin.

In my opinion, a grade A is not necessarily a better instructor than a grade B and you should not base your decision of instructor solely on their grade. Like all of us, we each perform differently in tests and this can affect our grade. Perhaps in addition to knowing their grade, you could ask about pass rates. Most good and conscientious instructors will be able to tell you.

REVIEWS

In this day and age, it's easy to get feedback on driving instructors via social media. Many driving instructors have a Facebook page, and some publish photos of successful students or write congratulating comments about their successful pupils. Remember though, there might be bad reviews too. But, if you want to know why the review was not great, you could phone the instructor or message them and ask them about it. Or send a private message to the reviewer. Some reviews can be spiteful and could be more to do with the student's attitude than the quality of the instructor.

WHO EMPLOYS DRIVING INSTRUCTORS?

There are independent instructors and those that work as a franchisee for a franchise company such as The AA, BSM or Red. Many however are independent. The one thing that almost driving instructors have in common is that they are self employed, even those that work for a franchise.

Driving Instructors don't earn a salary, so their income comes from you, the student. When you book your lessons make sure you can commit to what you are booking. Every time slot filled in an Instructors diary is precious. When a person cancels at short notice or doesn't't show for their lesson then that's a loss of income for the instructor.

An instructor is responsible for paying for their own car, car insurance, servicing costs, fuel, franchise fees, their ADI licence, continual professional development (CPD), training as well as their own household bills.

So, whoever you choose for your driving lessons please be respectful and give as much notice as possible if you need to change or cancel a lesson.

3.
THE THEORY TEST

The driving test is spilt into two parts. The theory test and the practical test. With good preparation, you can ace the theory test and the practical test. I mention this now as over the years many students delay booking a theory test.

You do not need to pass your theory test before starting your driving lessons. Some people do like to however, taking lessons with a professional instructor can help you prepare for your theory test. You will be putting the theory that you learn into practice and applying it to real life situations on the roads. It is also an ideal environment to ask your instructor questions based on the theory that you have been learning as you begin to put your theory knowledge into practice.

So, let's talk about the theory test. You cannot book and take a practical test until you have passed the theory test so it's kind of important.

My advice would be to get this done as soon as possible. Over the years I have had many students who put off taking the theory test.

They have lots of excuses too. Here are a few;

- Oh, I've been so busy with college/work
- I just don't seem to have the time
- I'm going to book it tonight (they never do)
- I have no money
- My parents are paying, and they haven't booked it yet.

These are just a few reasons. Hardly anyone mentions that they are anxious about the test. Or worried that they might fail. I think that these feelings do play a big part in why some students delay revising and booking their theory test. I'm sure that you could think of other reasons.

> **!** ***A note about anxiety*** — *It is natural to be anxious about taking any type of test. Talk to your instructor about how you are feeling about the theory test. Ask for help. Revising for your theory test is a very personal thing and often driving instructors don't get too involved. But they are there to help. Talk to them about any concerns you have, or any areas of theory that you are struggling with. Remember, they aren't't just there to help you pass the practical test.*

If you take too long booking, taking and passing your theory test then you can take much longer to learn to drive and pass the practical test. The longer you put off booking it, the greater your nerves and anxiety might become. This in turn could cost you more money and increase the level anxiety of the practical driving test.

Recently, someone told me that they were desperate to pass their driving test. They had been learning for 5 months and were not far off being ready for their practical test. But they hadn't even booked or taken a theory test yet!

Remember, most driving test centres have a waiting list of available times for the theory test and practical test. This can vary from a few days to a few months. The longest I have known for a practical test is 26 weeks! Thankfully, at time of writing, this is no longer the case, but it can change at any time.

To pass the theory test you need to obtain 43/50 for the theory questions and then 44/75 for the hazard perception element of the test.

To be honest, the theory test is not that difficult so long as you put the time and effort in and revise. There are many apps available now for revising the theory test, but, a word of warning, the apps alone will not help you to pass.

Some are free and others will need to paid for. The old adage, you get what you pay for is certainly true when it comes to theory revision apps. A little investment now could save the cost of a retest.

You should become familiar with the Highway Code. The information contained in the Highway Code is important for every driver. Ignorance is no excuse when it comes to the law. Other books on your reading list should be

"Know your Traffic Signs" and "Driving-The Essential Skills."

I appreciate that revising for anything can be boring and for some it is challenging too. So, be smart about how you revise. Short periods of revision are best. No more than 20 minutes at a time, then take a break. Our brains work best and retain information when learning in short bursts. If you aim to do an hours revision a day as a minimum, then three 20 minute sessions could be the perfect way to gain that knowledge.

As soon as you know that you will be learning to drive then start preparing. You don't need to wait until your 17th birthday to start revising. In fact, you can start as soon as you can read! Parents can encourage their children on car journeys to identify road signs or point out signs. I used to do this with my children and their knowledge is now excellent. Another excellent way of encouraging observation skill is to count motorbikes or cyclists on car journeys. This also plants a good message to the young driver to be, look out for those most vulnerable. My parents used to get my brother and I to play pub cricket. Counting the number of legs on a pub sign. For example, the Horse and Groom would be 6 points (6 legs). The point of these games is to help with observational skills. All of which will be useful when you eventually start driving.

Some elements of the theory which are often overlooked and not revised well are;

- ☐ - First Aid
- ☐ - Motorways
- ☐ - Documentation
- ☐ - Trams
- ☐ - Road works
- ☐ - Eco driving
- ☐ - Electronic devices and driving

You see, the theory covers everything you might need to know. There are regular revisions to the Highway Code too, so check online for latest changes or talk to your driving instructor.

Booking the theory test should only be done when you feel confident that you can pass it. Be aware of some sites that will charge you more for booking the theory test and offer a free second test. In my opinion, it's not worth it, especially as you will revise well and not need a second

test! This is the link that you will need to book your theory test.
https://www.gov.uk/book-theory-test

❗ *A note about specific learning needs - If you have a specific learning need, such as dyslexia for example, then it is worth mentioning this when booking. In most cases you will be given more time to complete the theory test.*

On the day of your theory test, make sure you are at the theory test centre 15 minutes before your test time. You will need to register and place your personal possessions into a secure locker. You **must take your driving licence with you** to your theory test appointment, and your confirmation email. Without your driving licence you will not be able to take the test, even if you have booked it. Your licence is your identification. Make sure too, that your address is up to date. If it is not, I would suggest that you update your licence before going to your theory test. This way it's ready for when you take your practical test too.

❗ *Old Paper Licences - If you happen to still have the old style paper provisional licence only, (highly unlikely that any of these remain) then please take a passport with you for photo ID.*

When you are shown to your PC and have been shown how to use the controls you need, take a deep breath and remember to take your time in completing the test.

You will get plenty of time, (57 minutes) so there is no need to rush. You can flag questions and come back to them later. This is a good technique and allows you to answer those you are 100% certain of and then return to those that you feel less confident about when you have more time.

The hazard perception element of the test is after the main set of questions.

There are 14 clips and 15 hazards to spot. So, this means that one of the clips will have two hazards in it.

A hazard can be defined as something on the road that would make you alter your direction or speed.

The hazard perception element is where you identify hazards by clicking a mouse button. The mouse does not need to be moved onto the hazard. You should think of the mouse button as your steering wheel or brake pedal. You only need click when you see something that might make you want to alter your direction or speed. Or if you like, STOP, SLOW DOWN, SWERVE or SWEAR!

If you have done sufficient revision and preparation, then you should pass the theory at the first attempt. But, don't worry if you are not successful. Simply book again and revise the elements that you were less aware of. You will receive a document that tells which areas you were weaker in. Sadly, it does not say the exact questions you got wrong. But, don't be disheartened. Book it again and revise more.

If you have passed, then congratulations! You can either continue with your driving lessons or begin the process of looking for a driving instructor.

Remember to keep your pass certificate somewhere safe. It has a unique number on it which you might need when booking your practical test.

4.
THE PRACTICAL TEST

The practical driving test has included many elements over the years. If you are learning with a family member or friend, then it's possible that they will be teaching you what they remember from when they learnt to drive.

In December 2017, the driving test changed. Certain elements were taken out and new elements were introduced.

The turn in the road (three point turn) and the reverse around a corner were both removed from the test. In their place were introduced driving forwards into a parking bay and reversing out. Also, pulling up on the right hand side of the road and then reversing up to two car lengths.

In addition, the independent section of the test increased from 10 minutes to 20 minutes. This part of the test now requires that you follow directions given to you by a Sat Nav or one in five test candidates will be asked to follow road signs.

Since the driving test changed, the feedback from pupils has been very positive. Many say how they like the independent part of the test.

WHAT SHOULD YOUR INSTRUCTOR BE TEACHING YOU ?

With the best will in the world, your driving instructor will not be able to teach you everything that you are likely to experience on the roads after you have passed your test. There is a syllabus that all driving instructors should be following though. Subject areas that your instructor should be including are: -

- Cockpit drill
- Mirror Signal Manoeuvre
- Moving off and stopping
- Correct use of signals
- Junctions - entering and emerging to the left
- Junctions - entering and emerging to the right
- Roundabouts
- Cross roads
- Emergency Stop
- Pedestrian crossings
- Rural Single Carriageways
- Country lanes
- Dual carriageway
- Motorways
- Reversing
- Turn in road (three point turn)
- Reverse bay park
- Forward bay park
- Parallel park
- Pull up on the right and move off safely
- Show and tell questions
- Use of a satellite navigation system
- Independent driving — following road signs

There are of course many other aspects to driving not listed above. And remember, simply covering all of the topics in the above list does not necessarily make you an excellent driver. What it will do however, is give you the base level of competence in order to take and pass a driving test.

You may hear family and friends tell you that you really start learning once you have passed your driving test. Well, there is some truth to this, but, if your driving instructor is thorough, then you should feel confident to drive anywhere after passing your test.

HOW LONG WILL IT TAKE FOR ME TO PASS MY TEST?

This is a great question! It's a bit like asking how long is a piece of string? The answer is we don't know. The DVSA suggests that around 40 hours of driving lessons with a professional instructor plus 60 hours of private practice is a good base from where to start. But this might not always be possible. There might be a cost implication, as well as finding a member of the family that is prepared to dedicate the number of hours necessary to get you to the correct standard. What I can tell you is this; those drivers who have supplemented their driving lessons with additional practice with family or friends often learn faster, gain more experience and become more confident and proficient drivers.

Every driver is different. Age can play a part in learning to drive. If your only source of learning will be with a driving instructor, then you could use the following as a guide.

Multiply your age by 1.5 to give you a minimum number of hours for a fast learner. So, for example, a 17 year old who picks things up quickly should anticipate, as a minimum 17 x 1.5 = 25.5 hours.

Someone starting later in life will require longer. Someone who is 30 should consider at least 45 hours of lessons as a minimum. But, as I have said, every driver is very different. I have had students who have passed after 10 hours of lessons and others that have taken 100 hours. I have found though, that the average number of hours for my students is around 35 - 40 regardless of age, which would imply that the DVSA are correct in their suggestion.

TO PASS THE DRIVING TEST

To pass the driving test you will need to commit no more than 15 driver faults. If you commit a serious or dangerous fault, then you will not pass.

The 3 types of faults you can make:

- a dangerous fault — this involves actual danger to you, the examiner, the public or property
- a serious fault — something potentially dangerous
- a driving fault — this is not potentially dangerous, but if you keep making the same fault, it could become a serious fault

WHY DO PEOPLE FAIL THEIR DRIVING TEST ?

Have you ever wondered what the top reasons are for failing the driving test? Well, here you have it, as recorded by the DVSA for the year 2019/2020, and in no particular order.

- Observation at Junctions
- Response to signs – Traffic lights
- Use of mirrors — changing direction
- Normal road positioning
- Steering control
- Safety when moving off
- Turning right at junctions
- Control when reverse parking
- Control when moving off
- Response to signals — traffic signs

What is interesting is that the top 10 reasons for failure of a driving test remain pretty consistent. Is this down to bad teaching, or nerves on the day?

I think what is clear here is that driving instructors can learn from this list as much as new drivers. It might be worth speaking with your instructor and working together to ensure that you aren't caught out by any of the above. Also, this list does not represent the only reasons why people fail.

How can you avoid failing for the reasons identified above?

In the following chapters I will explain how each one might occur and hopefully prevent you from making the errors that would cause you to collect a serious or dangerous fault.

5.
OBSERVATION AT JUNCTIONS

You would like to think that you would never exit a junction or turn into a junction if it was unsafe. So, why is this in the top 10 of reasons of why people fail their driving test?

As we read earlier, 95% of crashes are caused through driver error. In the case of junctions, it is most often down to poor observation from one or both drivers. The consequences of getting it wrong can be potentially catastrophic so it's no wonder that the examiner will be wanting to see you making full and effective observations at junctions.

I sometimes think that the decision a learner driver makes to go at a junction is down to their fear of not wanting to seem hesitant. Is this something you are thinking about at junctions? Do you believe that if you are hesitant you will fail? The reality is, if you happen to miss an opportunity to go, then, whilst it isn't ideal, you will most likely only receive a minor driver fault for this. If you are too brisk in your decision making and pull out in front of another vehicle, causing them to slow down then this is more likely to result in a serious or a dangerous fault.

It comes back to: -

"What would you do if you were on your own?"

There are various junction types and without wishing to complicate things, how you deal with each junction will be similar. Below are some of the junctions you should become familiar with if you don't want to fail your driving test.

- T Juntions
- Y Junction
- Crossroad

- ☐ Unmarked Crossroad/Junction
- ☐ Slip roads off Dual Carriageways/Motorways

You must be effective with your observations at junctions. You have an expectation of other road users to be looking out for you so in turn you must do the same.

I am not going to explain each one of these in turn as how you deal with each one doesn't really change. What does change is the environment where the junction is located. Instead I am going to try and make things simple.

Let us simplify junctions and look at the two key types that there are.

Simply put, there are OPEN junctions and CLOSED junctions

An open junction is one that affords you an excellent view of the road to both sides. There are no obstructions. But, don't be complacent. Even at open junctions it's easy to miss the obvious.

A closed junction is where your view is severely restricted. Extra caution is required here. Some closed junctions may be STOP junctions, and with good reason. So, take extra care. Edge your car forward (creep and peep) to gain a better view of the road and what is coming.

Junctions are where a majority of crashes occur so it's important to make **full and effective observations**. Think about the vulnerable road users such as cyclists, horse riders and pedestrians. Make sure you are 100% certain that it is safe before proceeding. 99% certain is not enough certainty to go.

Many drivers miss things at junctions. It has been found that when scanning the road to the left and the right, drivers quite often miss what is in their immediate field of view which is right in front of them. These are the drivers that end up explaining to a police officer that they had no idea the cyclist was there, or that that they didn't't see the pedestrian crossing the road, even when they were directly in front of them.

Car door pillars can obscure your view, so you might need to move your head to the left and right, around the pillars, and ensure that you have assessed the junction correctly and are ready to go.

Finally, once into your new road, check your centre and right mirror to ensure that there is nothing that will prevent you from being able to accelerate up towards an appropriate speed.

6.
RESPONSE TO SIGNS — TRAFFIC LIGHTS

Traffic lights can make a learner driver feel a little paranoid, more so when they are on their driving test. When should I stop? When should I go? I know that this would appear to be really simple to anyone who has already passed their test but, when under pressure during a driving test then the humble traffic light can become something more sinister than just a red, amber or green light.

You need to know the sequence of lights and where the traffic light is located. By this I mean is it one that controls traffic flow at a busy intersection or is it at a pedestrian crossing. It might even be temporary traffic lights in place for road works.

Signs on the approach to road works would usually give sufficient notice that traffic lights were imminent, yet it's surprising how many people still brake hard when they see them. The golden rule with temporary traffic lights is, unless you can see them you should assume that they are red and begin to ease of the gas in preparation to stop.

What is the sequence of lights? Do you know? If you see a steady amber light on the approach to the traffic lights, what colour comes next, red or green? If you see a flashing amber light does it mean proceed or does it mean plan to stop?

The sequence of lights at traffic intersections

Red - Red Amber - Green - Amber - Red

The most common traffic light where learner drivers fail is in my opinion are those at busy intersections.

As you approach the traffic lights your job as a driver is to consider what might happen next. You need to anticipate.

Anticipation is key here. When approaching traffic lights there are a few questions that you should be asking yourself

- How long have the lights been that colour for?
- If they changed back to red now, could I stop safely?
- If they change to green, will I be ready to move off again safely and without holding others up?

If the lights are red on the approach, then how long have they been red for? If they were red when you first noticed them then we refer to this as a stale red light. One that has been red for some time with a chance it might return to green. Never rush to a stop. What would be the point? You brake late and in turn drivers following you do as you do. You could end up too close to the vehicle ahead only to find that as soon as you have stopped the light changes back to green and you are left fumbling around looking for first gear or even forgetting that a lower gear is required. This inevitably causes a stall and then more panic can set in.

You should be anticipating the change back to green. Slowing down on the approach to a red light and selecting an appropriate gear ready to move off again without interrupting the flow of traffic.

If the light is green on the approach, then we should be anticipating the change to amber then to red. There will potentially be a point of no return, that point at which to stop could be more dangerous than to proceed. The highway Code Rule 175 states:

You MUST stop behind the white 'Stop' line across your side of the road unless the light is green. If the amber light appears you may go on only if you have already crossed the stop line or are so close to it that to stop might cause a collision.
Laws RTA 1988 sect 36 & TSRGD regs 10 & 36

It's important to be proactive when dealing with traffic lights and **not** reactive.

With the best will in the world, it's still possible to be at the light as it changes to amber. If you can stop safely then of course you should but, if you are so close to the stop line that to stop would cause you to effectively do an emergency stop, this could be dangerous.

Remember too, that the stop line is the first line, not the one after the area for cyclists. That area should be kept free. When the light goes back to green, ensure you check left door mirror and right door mirror before moving off. You are checking for cyclists on your left and mopeds, motorcycles on the right.

You also have the green filter arrow to look out for. These can show the driver that they are permitted to now turn left or right even though other traffic is still held on a red light.

Look out for the extra light on traffic lights. It will either be situated below the green light or to the left or right of the green light. It's easy to miss, especially when you are concentrating on trying to move off without stalling or remembering to use your handbrake. Not all junctions have them. You may have heard on your lessons or when with friends or family that other drivers offer a friendly toot of the horn to prompt a driver to go as their light has changed. You don't really want this happening on your test so do look out for the filter arrows. Become familiar with the junctions local to you that have these filter arrows.

What about traffic lights at pedestrian crossings?

Crossing controlled by lights are

- Pelican Crossing
- Puffin Crossing
- Toucan Crossing
- Equestrian (Pegasus) Crossing

The sequence of lights at Puffin, Toucan and Pegasus crossings are
Red - Red Amber - Green - Amber - Red

At a Pelican crossing then the sequence is
Red - Flashing Amber - Green - Steady Amber - Red

You may have already noticed on your lessons that once a pedestrian has pressed the button at a pedestrian crossing the lights can sometime change quickly.

A proactive driver will be looking for the potential of this happening. You should be scanning the road ahead looking for pedestrians and cyclists that could use the crossing ahead. Consider easing off the gas a little, consider that stopping might be required. But, be careful not to slow too much if the light is on green as following drivers could get annoyed.

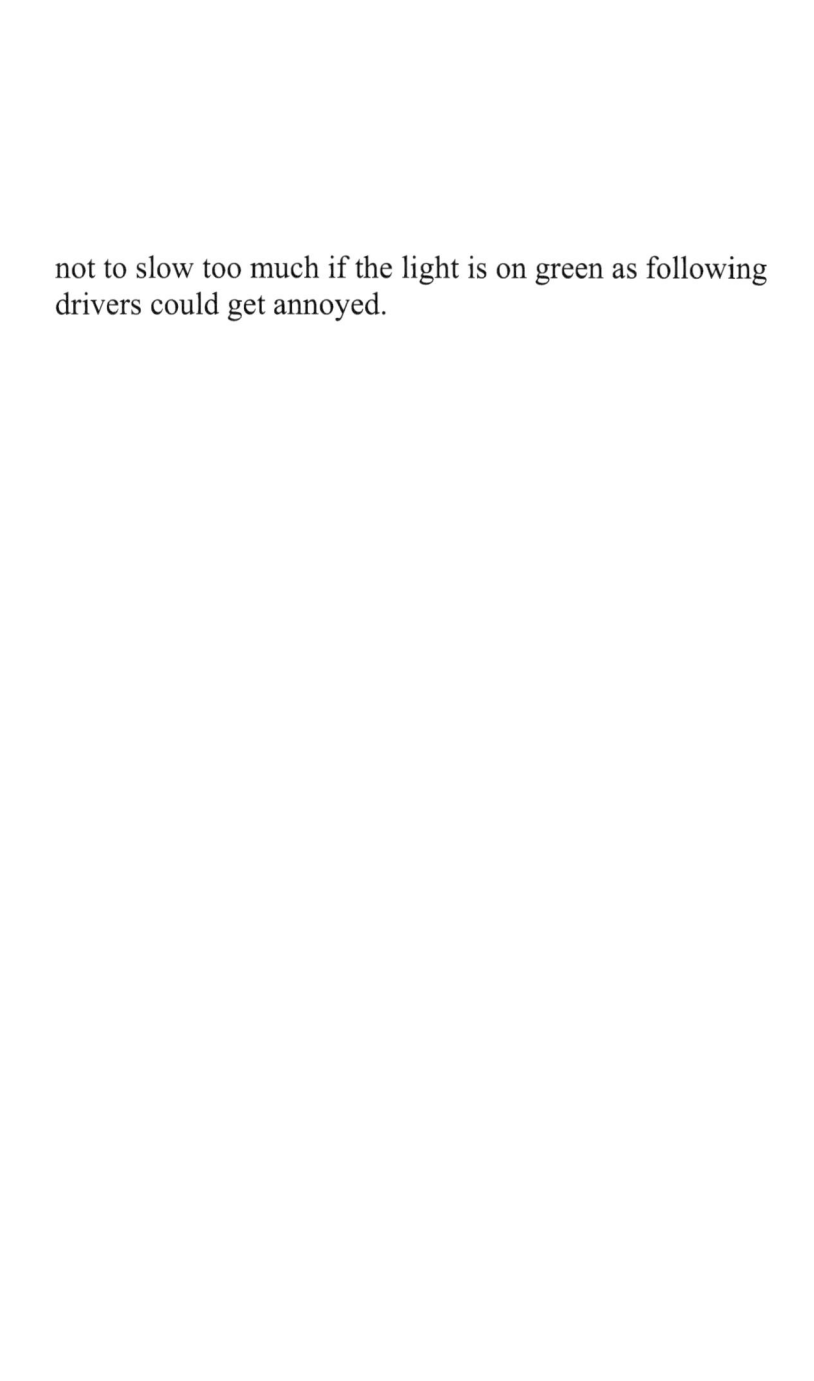

7.
USE OF MIRRORS

Mirrors, Mirrors, Mirrors!

Mirror Signal Manoeuvre (MSM) underpins the safety of everything that we do in driving. The use of the MSM routine would have been introduced to you on your very first lesson and most likely, every lesson since. It's the one thing that your driving instructor will be nagging you about right from your very first lesson.

Why are the mirrors there? Simply put, to keep you safe and those around you safe.

You have three mirrors to use. Two door mirrors and your centre mirror. The examiner will want to see you using your mirrors effectively whenever you change your speed or direction.

Mirrors should be used in pairs. You begin with the centre mirror then use a door mirror on the side of the car that relates to which direction you will be moving next.

OVERTAKING

As an example, if you are approaching a cyclist and preparing to pass them then you should be using your centre mirror and right door mirror on the approach to the cyclist ensuring that when you change direction, another vehicle isn't already doing that. Once you have passed the cyclist then you should check your centre mirror and left door mirrors to ensure adequate clearance has been given and that the cyclist is still riding and smiling.

CHANGING LANES

Other times when effective use of mirrors is important are when you are changing lanes. Without effective use of mirrors, you could cause a crash.

On a driving test it is not uncommon for the student driver to be in the wrong lane. Often, there is a sense of urgency that you need to move to another lane. If this is done without any use of mirrors it can result in a serious or dangerous fault and consequently, a fail.

CHANGING SPEED

What types of things on the road could cause you to slow the vehicle down or speed up?

- [ ] Speed limit changes
- [ ] Buses pulling in or out
- [ ] Cyclists
- [ ] Horses and riders
- [ ] Passing a school
- [ ] A blue light vehicle
- [ ] Potholes
- [ ] Blind bends

This is not an exhaustive list. What else can you think of? When you slow down you need to be aware of what is following you. How you use your brake when slowing will be determined by how close the following vehicle is. You certainly would not want to be braking hard if there is a car within a few metres of your rear bumper. Equally, if the vehicle behind is further back, knowing this can give you more time to brake and in doing so allow your brake lights to be seen for longer. This is good thing. The longer your brake lights are on then the safer you should be.

When you speed up, you should check your interior mirror followed by your right door mirror. You are looking to ensure that no other vehicle is about to pass you. The last thing you want is to find yourself in a drag race as you and the other driver try and reach the posted speed limit. Knowing that the other driver is passing means that you can ease of your gas pedal and allow them to pass before speeding up again.

Checking your mirrors when slowing down? How close is the vehicle behind you? How much time do you need to brake?

I often get asked if it's OK to wear sunglasses, or if you have to make obvious head movements. The answer is yes, you can wear sunglasses and no, you do not need to make obvious and exaggerated head movements to demonstrate that you are checking your mirrors.

Examiners are well trained, and they will know when you are or are not checking your mirrors.

8.
POSITIONING — NORMAL DRIVING

The examiner will want to see that you can position your vehicle correctly in the road. Your road position might change depending upon what type of road you are on. Your road position is important for your own safety and the safety of other road users.

A good road position will most often be in the centre of your lane however, occasionally you may adjust your position in order to obtain a better view of the road ahead. An example of this is when approaching some parked vehicles on your side of the road. It would be prudent to move the vehicle slightly to the right to get the better view. REMEMBER to check your mirrors when changing your position on the road.

I often see learner drivers approaching right hand bends on country lanes too close to the centre of the road. These types of road are narrower and require you to position differently. Too far to the middle and you could end up meeting another road user head on. Too far to the left and you might find yourself scraping the hedgerow or hitting those potholes

Faults for position in normal driving are generally because you have allowed the car to move too far to the right causing oncoming drivers to alter their direction or slow down to avoid you. Or, it might mean that you have moved too far to the left, perhaps so close to the curb or verge, that you are at risk of hitting it, mounting it or cause a risk to pedestrians or other road users.

On dual carriageways, you need to ensure that you do not drift into another lane or indeed straddle the lines in the middle of the road.

Distraction is a common factor leading to the collection of a serious or dangerous fault in this category.

Perhaps you were looking down at your speedometer when you should have been concentrating on the road ahead. Maybe whilst you were demonstrating one of the show me questions you were looking at switches and buttons instead of the road. It can be so easy to drift off line under these circumstances. To avoid this from happening, become familiar with the location of the switches in your instructor's car and in your own vehicle.

You might think that you have only taken your eyes off the road for a second, but, a second at 30mph is a long way and this distance increases the faster you are going.

Of course you should be keeping an eye on the speed limits, and you should also be able to operate certain controls without this effecting your road position, so, the best way to do this is to check your speedometer when you are in a straight line and not as you are about to enter or exit a bend in the road.

You will hear the examiner say at the beginning of the Show Me question *"**when it is safe to do so, show me…**"*

This means that they are looking for you to know when the correct time for doing such a task is. This would be when your vehicle is pointing in a straight line.

Distracted driving is a factor in many crashes. Using a mobile phone or adjusting something on your media centre/radio or CD Player. These are just some of the reasons why people fail to maintain proper road position.

9.
STEERING CONTROL

H ands follow eyes!

They do, it's true! If you look somewhere you can be sure that your hands will follow.

A serious or dangerous fault in this category is often caused when the driver has taken their eye off where they want to go and has instead looked at something else. For example, turning right into a junction and a car is waiting to exit the same junction. I have seen students being too busy watching the other vehicle that they have failed to straighten up in time and consequently started to steer onto the opposite side of the road. We call this a swan neck.

Other times, perhaps watching a pedestrian on the pavement instead of the road they are entering and then they end up steering towards that pedestrian.

Sometimes a steering fault can be collected when emerging out of a junction. Especially those junctions that are quite square. By this I mean, where the pavement forms a right angle to the end of the road. If you position your vehicle too close to the left side on these types of junctions then as you emerge left, the rear wheels could mount the curb. Sometimes this is just marked as a minor driver fault, but it does depend on how much of the wheel went up onto the pavement.

At roundabouts for example, when turning left. If you leave your observations too late then you might be looking to your right when you are supposed to be steering left. This is quite common and results in the driver drifting away from their normal position on the road and having to bring the steering back quite sharply to correct where they are on the road, or the examiner has to do it for you!

You need to look well ahead and plan for potential obstructions. You should create a driving plan that will allow you to consider the best approach and road position for any hazard you might encounter. Parked cars, cyclists, junctions, roundabouts to name but a few. Focus on being more proactive in your driving and less reactive.

Failing to plan is planning to fail!

10.
SAFETY WHEN MOVING OFF

Quite simply, this is about effective observations.

People who fail for this reason would not have made good observations before moving away either from the side of the road or perhaps out of a parking space. Moving off safely is one of the first things you would have learned from your instructor when starting your lessons.

I like to think that when moving away from the left side of the road you should remember to check left to right. **Always look last in the direction you are about to move**. So do your checks in this order; *left blind spot, left* *door mirror, centre mirror, the road ahead, right door mirror and right blind spot.* If all is clear then you can begin to move away but remember, as you begin to move off, do a final quick check over the right shoulder, just in case. I call this the lucky seven. Motorcyclists call it their lifesaver check. It could be yours too!

If you pull away and cause another driver to alter their direction or speed through lack of effective observations, then you can expect to pick up a serious fault and fail your driving test. Remember, after you have pulled away then you must try gain speed briskly (not aggressively) so as not to cause other drivers to slow down, especially when moving away on a hill. An early gear change from first to second on a hill could reduce your speed significantly causing following drivers to have to slow down or you might even stall.

11.
TURNING RIGHT AT JUNCTIONS

This could either be for emerging out of a junction or turning right into a junction. When emerging consider if the junction is open or closed. (see Chapter 5).

If the junction is a STOP junction, then make sure you have stopped completely before edging forward. Stopping completely does not mean that you need to apply the handbrake, but your wheels MUST stop turning. I find that stopping and counting "1001, 1002" is usually sufficient.

Think about your road position in relation to the width of the road, road markings and any obstructions, such as parked vehicles. Will your road position have the potential to impact on any other road user? When emerging out of the junction, ensure you have made effective observations so that when you pull away you do not cause another road user to stop, slow down, swerve or swear! Remember the vulnerable road users such as cyclists and motorcyclists.

When turning right into a junction remember you are crossing traffic and any oncoming traffic has priority over you. You will need to assess the space that you have, and the time it will take you to turn into the new road.

Make sure you have used the correct mirrors before signaling and then your road position must be near to the centre of the road but not over the centre line. You should position to take into account any obstructions, such as parked vehicles.

Judging when to turn can be tricky, especially when under pressure from being on a driving test. When you are assessing the turn ask yourself, would I have enough time to cross the road on foot? If the answer is yes, then you most likely have time to cross in the car.

"what would I do if I was on my own?"

Don't rush and don't be concerned about being hesitant. The examiner will know if the time you choose to go is appropriate.

Don't forget the door pillars. In many cars they can be an obstruction to a good view either in or out of a road, so move your head around a bit. Make sure you are certain that there is no danger before making your turn.

12.
CONTROL - WHEN REVERSE PARKING

This is either a bay park (forward or backward) or a parallel park. It could also be the straight line reverse you would be required to do after the pulling up on the right exercise.

REVERSE BAY PARK

Let's deal with bay park first. The observations that you make are as important as the control over the vehicle.

Vehicle control is about your use of low speed and your accuracy at the end of the park.

Select the bay you are going to reverse into. DO NOT RUSH! Which bay would you choose if you were on your own? Slow and steady will always win the day. Your goal is to be between the lines. Do not worry if you are closer to one line than the other. Do not worry if you are not completely straight and do not worry if it's not perfect at the first attempt. You can always shunt forward and back again. Use careful clutch control and if necessary, adjust the mirrors to gain a better view of your position in the bay. When you have finished, if you want to open your door and have a look, do! That's what most full licence holders would do. If you are not in the bay to your satisfaction then make effective observations, move slowly forward until you feel you are now in a better position to tidy it up. Know what position your steering wheel is in and know when your wheels are straight.

FORWARD BAY PARK

During your driving test you might be asked by the examiner to enter a car park and choose a bay on the left or right that you can drive forward into. They will expect you to finish between the lines and NOT to drive straight through a bay into the one in front of it.

I have seen many students rush this exercise and panic as they wrongly believe that the examiner is expecting them to do the park as soon as the instruction is given. They have then, without much thought, driven into one of the first bays that they see. Often too quickly and certainly without any level of accuracy or control.

As with the reverse bay park, effective observations are important. Don't just drive forwards into a bay without first checking your mirrors. Think about the mirrors you would check if you were making a left or a right turn. Do the same for the forward bay park. Mirror - Signal - Manoeuvre. You need to give information to anyone that may have followed you into the car park.

The examiner is not interested in your method of doing the bay park. They don't care if you count lines or wait until the white line is in a specific place in relation to your door mirror. All they want to see is a reasonably accurate forward bay park.

To ensure that this happens, you will need to slow down quite considerably. Use first gear and good clutch control. Similar to the type of clutch control you would use when creeping and peeping at a junction. As with the reverse bay park, do not worry if your car is not in the centre of the bay, or closer to one line than the other or indeed if you are a bit wonky in the bay. So long as you are between the lines, job done!

PARALLEL PARK

A good parallel park is as much about the observation as it is about the control. Take your time.

What is your objective for the parallel park? Quite simply, it's to finish the manoeuvre, reasonably close to the curb and no more than two car lengths from the vehicle ahead of you. The examiner should tell you that you can ignore driveways for the purpose of the exercise

Everyone has a slightly different method but it's not the method that the examiner is watching. It's the end result they are interested in. How you achieve that is really up to you.

You need to be reasonably close to the curb. If necessary, adjust your left mirror to get a better view of the curb (remember to put it back afterwards). And then move the vehicle slowly. This is not a timed exercise, so don't rush. Slow and steady is best.

At the end, if you feel the need to adjust your position on the road slightly, then do. Shunt forward and backwards to get closer to the curb. 15 cm away is ideal but don't be too concerned if it's a little bit more, but not too much more. Remember this is a parking exercise and your car should finish in a position you would be happy to leave it in.

Full and effective observations are important on any of the manoeuvres. If you are not completely accurate, you can always shunt forward or backward to correct, but you don't get a second chance to look!

PULL UP ON THE RIGHT AND REVERSE BACK

I often get asked why this needs to be done. It does say in the highway code that parking on the right hand side

should be avoided however, it is something which is actually quite commonly used by many types of driver for different reasons. For example, ambulance driver, delivery drivers, postal workers to name but a few.
Highway Code Rule 239

You will most likely be asked to do this manoeuvre when the examiner can see that you have sufficient space to do it. As with all the manoeuvres DO NOT RUSH!

Your instruction will be similar to this

"Please find a safe place on the right hand side to pull up and stop"
I advise my students to think of this manoeuvre similarly to a right turn. The MSM routine is the same as is your road position. Whilst waiting to turn, should oncoming traffic prevent you from doing so be patient and wait. Learners tell me how they don't like the idea of holding traffic up and this is a cause of them rushing. This can be to their detriment as t turning across the road, causing oncoming vehicles to slow down is never a good choice and will almost certainly lead to a fail.

Once your location is chosen, give yourself some room to allow yourself to position your vehicle reasonably close to the curb on the other side. You want to try and avoid too much steering. If you try to pull across the road almost opposite where you want to stop, you could end up clipping the curb or stopping with the rear of the car poking out into the road. If you do find that this has happened, wait for any oncoming vehicles to pass and if it's safe to do so, move forward to straighten up the car. You don't want to be reversing if the rear of the car is not parallel with the curb.

Once you are happy with your position the examiner will then ask you to reverse back up to two car lengths. They should advise that you can ignore any driveways for the purpose of this part of the exercise.

Students who fail this exercise for control either move out into the road or get too close to the curb and hit it. It is quite easy to mount the payment on this manoeuvre, especially if you are near a dropped curb. So, for this reason, be aware of what's behind you on your right side as well as your left side.

Keep your wheels straight. Move the car slowly and make good use of all round observation. You can use your right mirror to gauge your accuracy but don't stare in it to the expense of looking elsewhere.

13.
CONTROL - WHEN MOVING OFF

Yet again, control comes up as a reason why people fail their driving tests.

This time it is about stalling when moving off. This could be at junctions, on a hill or simply from the side of the road. There are a number of times during the test that you will be asked to pull over and stop in a safe and convenient place. You will then be asked to move off when it's safe to do so. This is where the control element comes in. Can you move off without stalling? It's worth knowing that one stall does not generally mean you have failed. It all depends on whether or not you have impeded the flow of traffic or stalled in a way that causes other drivers to slow down, stop or alter their direction to get around you.

Let's look at the three main areas of stalling. Once you have stopped at the side of the road place the car and neutral and put on the handbrake. It doesn't matter which order you do this in. But it will avoid you trying to move off again in the wrong gear.

MOVING OFF - FROM THE SIDE OF THE ROAD

Prepare - Observe - Move. Prepare your car by ensuring you are in the correct gear to move off, usually first. Find your biting point if this is what you normally do, hand on hand brake, observe around the car and ensure you have sufficient time to move off without impacting upon the flow of traffic behind you. When you are ready, release the handbrake and move off, (you may want to consider if a signal is appropriate at this point) raising your clutch smoothly as you begin to accelerate. As your clutch comes up revs drop, so we need to compensate for this by accelerating. DON'T FORGET your blind spot check as you move off.

Common reasons for not moving off under control in this situation could be trying to move off in 2nd or 3rd or trying to rush away and raising the clutch too fast and stalling, thereby impeding the traffic flow. Remember, take your time and things should be just fine.

MOVING OFF - ON A HILL

Follow the procedure above but remember, you may need a higher biting point and more revs. Some modern cars are now fitted with a feature called hill start assist. This feature is permitted to be used. Ask you instructor if their car has it and how to use it properly.

The difference between moving away from the side of the road on the flat and on a hill is that, on a hill, you will need more gas, and don't be too quick moving from first gear to second. Too soon and the car could stall or dramatically slow down. Hills vary in steepness but, I have found that accelerating up to between 15 and 18 mph before moving from first gear to second prevents the likelihood of a stall or causing following drivers having to slow down.

MOVING OFF - AT JUNCTIONS

Make sure you have sufficient time to be able to pull out of the junction and get up to speed without slowing down other traffic. If you rush, you are more likely to stall (lack control) and depending upon your position when you stall might collect a serious fault, specifically if your car has crossed the Give Way / STOP line.

MOVING OFF - AT ROUNDABOUTS

It's very common for a stall to happen when at roundabouts. The learner driver is desperately trying not to hold up the driver behind that when they see a gap, they rush their clutch up and stall.

You do not need to rush at roundabouts. Of course, you don't want to be stuck there forever either. Watch the traffic, like you do on your lessons. Look at the other vehicles for signals, road position and where the wheels of the other cars are pointing. Look at the driver too. Beware the signals though, are they genuine?

I often get told by learner drivers how nervous roundabouts make them feel. I understand this. It's because you fear stalling in the path of another vehicle. But why are you on your test? Your driving instructor and you have agreed that you are ready for your test. This means that you both feel that you are ready to be on the road as an independent driver. It also means that during your lessons you have demonstrated sufficient ability at roundabouts to warrant booking a driving test.

If you are lacking confidence at roundabouts then you should ask yourself, why have you booked your driving test. Your instructor is there to help and support you. If roundabouts make you nervous then perhaps you need to focus on these and get as much practice as you can.

14.
RESPONSE TO SIGNALS — TRAFFIC SIGNS

These are the road signs or road markings that tell you to do or not do something.

Consider where these might be. If you think about road signs, you should be looking for signs painted on the road that tell you to do something. For example, keep left or keep right, STOP or Give Way. Keep Clear signs and box junctions. All of these could give reason for the examiner to fail you if you do not follow the rules given by the signs that you see as described by the Highway Code.

I have seen students fail their driving test for not stopping at a STOP junction. They would insist that they did, but the law is clear. The vehicle must stop at the STOP line. This means zero movement of the wheels. You must stop behind the line and then, creep and peep if required to obtain a better view.

If the wheels rotate even a fraction, then the examiner will consider you to have NOT stopped and you will receive a serious driving fault. I am often asked if you need to apply the handbrake in this situation. Well, the simple answer is no. Applying the handbrake is not necessary provided that the vehicle has stopped. However, you might want to consider applying the handbrake as there can then be no doubt in your mind or that of the examiner that you did not stop.
Highway Code Rule 171

WARNING - *Do not attempt to apply the handbrake before the car has stopped! This can result in a sudden stop, no brake lights would be displayed and, as a consequence, a following driver could run into the back of your vehicle. Always ensure that your vehicle has stopped* *by applying the footbrake first then once stationery, apply the handbrake.*

Worded road markings such as KEEP CLEAR are there to prevent the blockage of regularly used entrances and exits. In order to help the flow of traffic a KEEP CLEAR will be painted on the road to help a local business or car park.
Know Your Traffic Signs, Page 71

Box junctions are those areas of yellow hatch markings located on an area that you should not enter unless your exit is clear. *Highway Code Rule 174*

Keep left and keep right signs help the driver know where to position their vehicle. You can find these where the road splits from single carriageway to dual carriageway, or at a roundabout or even at traffic lights. They are designed to help although, most drivers tend not to need them as they gain experience although, I have found them useful, especially when driving around an unfamiliar town or city.

Solid white lines should not be crossed. Know the rules surrounding what you can and cannot overtake on a solid white line. *Highway Code Rule 129*

Areas of white diagonal striped lines, sometimes referred to as hatched markings or chevrons, painted onto the road are there to divide the lanes and protect vehicles that are turning right. You can enter the hatched area provided that the line surrounding the hatched area is broken and you do not cause danger to other road users. If the line is solid, then you MUST NOT enter the hatched area. *Highway Code Rule 130*

Turning right at the end of a one-way street is another way in which a road sign can help you. A common reason for failing here is that the student driver will often still position to the left as they would normally do. Being a one-way street, theoretically nobody should enter into the one way street from the end you are exiting at. Therefore, follow the usual MSM routine and position your car to the right hand side of the road on your approach to the junction. Turning right from the left side on this occasion will most likely result in a serious fault and a fail. *Highway Code Rule 143*

15.
OTHER COMMON PITFALLS

EFFECTIVE OBSERVATION WHEN REVERSING

So many students I teach find this difficult to do. They feel that they are looking through the rear window for no particular reason. Well, what do you think could be behind you?

In a car park, people walk behind reversing cars. It doesn't seem a logical thing to do but they do. Looking in your mirrors only will NOT necessarily alert you to this in time.

In a parallel park manoeuvre, or pulling up on the right, rear observations are important to assess the curbs and anyone coming from the rear, perhaps from a driveway.

Reversing out of a parking space. Your mirrors will not cover everything. You should make effective observations through the rear window to ensure you have covered everything and that you and other road users are safe.

When reversing, I have found that the reason students are not looking enough, is down to reversing too quickly. Although they feel they are going slowly it's generally not slow enough to ensure full and effective observations.

Hesitancy

What does it mean to be hesitant? Many students fail because they rush away at a junction or cross the path of another vehicle forcing them to slow down. They tell me that they didn't want to be seen as hesitant. Well, being safe is not being hesitant.

If you miss numerous safe opportunities to go, then of course a serious fault would be recorded against you. You have held up traffic unnecessarily.

You should always be ready to move away from junctions as soon as it is safe and correct to do so.

MAKING PROGRESS

What does it mean to make progress in a driving situation? To pass your driving test you need to be able to demonstrate that you can drive at a speed that is realistic to the road and traffic conditions. Hazards should be approached at a safe and controlled speed without being over cautious or hindering the progress of other road users. If you drive too slowly then this can cause dangers for you and for other road users

APPROPRIATE SPEED

What is appropriate speed? When you see a National Speed Limit sign does that automatically mean you should do 60mph? Think about where you are when you see these signs. You might be driving through a village subject to a 30mph limit then are asked to turn into a country lane. At some point you may see a National Speed Limit sign. Does this mean you should now speed up? I have had students who believe that they must now put their foot down and do a faster speed even though their view of the road ahead is restricted. Their only explanation for doing this is that they think that they will fail if they don't do the speed limit. WRONG! An examiner is looking for you to demonstrate your ability to judge what is an appropriate speed for the environment you are in. The easiest way for you to ensure you drive at an appropriate speed is to think

"Can I stop safely in the distance that I can see to be clear?"

If your answer is no then you need to think about what a safe speed would be. Imagine how quickly you could respond if there was a tractor around the next bend!
Highway Code Rules 144, 146, 147

STOPPING ON THE LEFT

During the course of your driving test you will be asked to stop somewhere safely on the left at least three times. Five times if you include the hill start and the angled start. The examiner is looking for you to find a safe location where stopping would not impede the flow of traffic.

Remember, the examiner is not trying to trick you and there is no hidden agenda. They are NOT trying to catch you out. They would not ask you to do this if they considered that the road you are on to be unsafe. I like to call this a SCALP place! A **S**afe, **C**onvenient **A**nd **L**egal **P**lace.
When you receive the instruction from the examiner to find a safe place to pull up on the left, follow the MSM routine. Look ahead and determine a suitable place to stop. These are just some of the areas you should avoid.

- Driveways
- Bus Stops
- Stopping within 10 metres of a junction
- Cycle Lanes (unless outside its hours of operation)
- Bus Lanes (unless outside its hours of operation)
- Double Yellow / Single Yellow Lines / Red Routes

Can you think of anymore?

Once you have stopped safely, apply the hand brake and place the car into neutral. It's very common for students to stop and leave the car in second or third gear and then try to move off again, in that gear, and stalling. Stalling once isn't an issue, but remember, this is a test. A stall on a test doesn't make you fail, but it can make you panic!

Keep calm, check that you are in the correct gear by placing it in neutral and resulting first gear. Make you full and effective observations again and when it is safe to do so, move away.

16.
MANAGING TEST DAY NERVES

I have found over the years that candidates going to their driving test are either excited, calm or extremely nervous.

How do you cope with those nerves on your test?

On the run up to your driving test you will hear from many people about how all you need to do is stay calm and you will be fine. Well, that easy for them to say isn't it? They aren't the ones doing the test. How can you manage your own nerves leading up to the test and on the day itself?

PREPARATION

Preparation is key to having a good driving test. If you feel underprepared, then this will only lead you to feeling more anxious on the day of the test. ON the lead up to your test, begin to think about those areas that you feel less confident about. Speak with your instructor about these elements of your driving and use the time to practice these until you are feeling more confident.

THE MANOEUVRES

As my students get closer to their test day, we discuss what it is that worries them the most. Many of them tell me it's manoeuvres. This often takes me by surprise as in most cases I see that they are fine but, it is about confidence isn't it, so we will spend time doing manoeuvres to ensure that the student feels confident. BUT! Sometimes this can be detrimental to other aspects of their driving. Let me put it this way. A manoeuvre takes about 2 minutes of the driving test, the remaining 38 - 40 minutes of the test is about driving, reading the road, observing speed limits, following a satellite navigation system or road signs. I am not suggesting for one moment you don't practice the manoeuvres but with a manoeuvre you can always take your time and make a correction if it's not gone white right. The same cannot be said for rest of the drive.

DEALING WITH OTHER'S STORIES

Everyone has a story to tell about their own driving test experience. Some of these are really positive stories and can help but often, the stories can be counter productive. They are told with the best of intentions but can have the opposite effect. This is YOUR test and no one else. Their experiences are not yours. When we listen to what others say we can believe falsely that we are going to have the same experience. It's time to switch off from others and focus instead on your own story.

URBAN MYTHS

Every driving test centre has "that examiner" who strikes fear into the heart of the test candidates. Without ever meeting the examiner it's easy to form an opinion of what the examiner is like. And when your name is called by that examiner your heart can sink. Examiners are just people doing a job. Believe it or not they want you to pass. So long as you deliver a safe drive there is no reason why you shouldn't. So right here and now, tell yourself that you won't have your opinion clouded by the thoughts and suggestions of others.

Another urban myth which has been doing the rounds since I was learning to drive over 30 years ago. This is the myth that examiners have to fail so many people each week.

I'm sure this myth was started by someone who felt that they should have passed their driving test but didn't. To make themselves feel better they made up this story.

Examiners will pass or fail you based on your performance, not because they haven't failed enough people that particular week.

CHOOSING THE DAY AND TIME OF YOUR TEST

Over the years I have analysed when my students do their driving tests. I have looked at the time of day, the day of the week, the time of year and can tell you that the only way to determine which day of the week and which time of the day is best for you is to consider what you are like as a person. Are you a morning person? Are you usually up at the crack of dawn and raring to go, or does it take you a while to get going? We are all different. If you are the type of person who really hates early mornings, then don't book the first test of the day. Think about when you feel awake and better able to concentrate.

Some people feel sleepy after they have had lunch. If this is you then book a test before lunch. Some feel they do their best work later in the day. Choose the time of day that suits you. As for which day of the week to choose, if you have a favourite day choose that. Not all test centres offer weekend tests so you might need to book a day off work or speak to a tutor about taking time away from a college or Uni course.

Being in control of the decision making for the time and day is important in helping you to manage those test day nerves.

CAN I SPEAK TO THE EXAMINER?

The answer is yes you can. Examiners that I have met are usually good judges of how a candidate is feeling and as such will do their best to put you at ease.

The first 5 minutes of the test are usually the settling in period for you. The examiner will give you some instructions to get you away from the test centre so you should expect them to be quiet at this point. They are not being rude or strict, simply giving you time to focus and concentrate.

Once they can see that you have settled in, they might open up conversation with you. They often show interest in your work, or college course you might be doing. It's not meant to distract you. So, continue to listen to any instructions they give you. If they have asked you a question and you need to concentrate, don't feel obliged to answer it. Focus on what needs to be done and, afterwards you can continue your conversation. The examiner will know you are not being rude.

SHOULD I TELL MY FRIENDS AND FAMILY

If you feel that the more people who know then the more nervous you will get then no, they don't need to know. It can be between you and your instructor. It's often a lovely surprise for family and friends when you show up waving a test pass certificate at them. Equally, if it's not gone so well then you can quietly get on with your day. I would say however, that confiding in a close friend or family member can be comforting. It's nice to know that you have someone to talk to about how you are feeling.

SHOULD I TAKE SOME CALMS?

When it comes to taking certain remedies to help calm your nerves then there is no harm at all, provided that they are legal of course. Just make sure you read the label.

There are plenty of other methods you can try. Meditation is a good way of helping calm your nerves. There is something called Thought Field Therapy (TFT) or Emotional Field Therapy (EFT) which works through tapping on various pressure points and of course there is hypnotherapy.

Once you have invested so much time and money into passing your driving test it can be a good idea to invest that little extra in some additional support.

To say thank you for downloading or purchasing this book here is a link to a sound cloud hypnosis script. Its designed to help calm your nerves on test day. Help you feel calm.

When you listen to it, find somewhere quiet where you will not be disturbed. Use some headphones and allow yourself to drift off. Hypnosis does not require you to have to focus on the words that are said, you simply need to relax and let the words drift over you. Even if you fall asleep you will benefit from the hypnotic experience.

https://soundcloud.app.goo.gl/DJ1EACUp2H15jB6i9

17.
AFTER THE DRIVING TEST

Congratulations! Yes! You have passed your driving test! All that hard work has paid off and you have demonstrated your skill at being a competent driver.

Now, I don't want to pour cold water on your amazing achievement but; you should remember that the level of pass you have achieved is the base level of requirement for driving on the roads. You can now drive on any road in the country and in any town or city in any car you can afford and at the posted speed limits.

What does this base level mean? Well, grab a pen and paper. Now jot down the number of hours of driving you have done to get to this point of a pass. Include private practice with family and friends as well as the lessons with your instructor. Now take that figure and divide by 24. The result is the number of days driving experience you have.

If we take the DVSA example of 40 hours of driving lessons plus 60 hours of private practice, then that's 100 hours! Sounds a lot doesn't't it? Well, that's only 4 days. That's right, 4 days! Not much is it? And that's if you have stuck to the recommended number of lessons. But, how many don't?

I recently had a student who had about 18 hours with me and similar in private practice. Now, he could do everything competently with me sat next to him to the point I thought, well, he could pass a test, and he wanted to "get it done." So, I now have to juggle my thoughts about the fact that he has not had nearly enough experience versus the fact that he is limited for funds. I knew he was capable so thought right, we will book the test and I'll work on the attitude. He passed first time with just 4 driver faults. Two days later, he had written his car off. Thankfully, there were no injuries. What else could I have done to ensure this did not happen? The answer is nothing. I could have suggested that he didn't do his test, but the chances are he would have done it anyway, using his own car. Driving instructors can advise the best course of action to follow. Do pay attention to the experience of an instructor. That said, we can advise against a student doing a test, but they do it anyway. An examiner has no way of knowing the number of lessons test candidate has had.

Once the student has passed then, they are on their own. They can now make decisions and choices on their own. Would more hours have made a difference in the situation I described above? Most certainly. Would he pay for more? No! So, until the law is changed to ensure that students take a minimum number of hours of professional tuition, incidents like this will remain commonplace.

So, what can YOU do to gain the valuable experience you will need to drive in all types of situations?

Passing the test and being able to drive in all areas takes time and more practice in order to gain experience. The more hours of driving you do the more competent you become. And the reason for this is simple. More experience, more knowledge and a greater ability to tackle the everyday problems that arise. Things that you might not experience on your driving lessons. Think of every mile you drive as depositing knowledge into your driving experience bank account. Over time, you might need to make a withdrawal of that knowledge.

PASS PLUS

Pass Plus used to be a great way of gaining valuable experience and reducing your insurance premiums. It's still a great way of gaining more experience and although it doesn't't necessarily lead to cheaper insurance, it could just go that extra step to help you avoid an accident.

ADVANCED DRIVING

Sadly, many people believe that you need to be old to do any sort of advanced driving. And, let's face it, there are not many young people who don't think that they are excellent drivers.

Advanced driving does involve a test and a little more expense, but, when you consider the extra skills you will learn there is no denying that it could just save your life. Once you have joined a local advanced driving group your training is generally free and carried out in your own vehicle.

DON'T THINK YOU ARE BETTER THAN YOU ARE

OK, this is the big one. No one admits to being a bad driver. The fact is we are all someone else's bad driver. We all make mistakes, even those of us who have had plenty of driver training.

Know your limitations. Consider your speed for the situation and environment you are in. If something happens can you stop safely?

I trust that reading through these pages has given you a better understanding of what is required to be successful on your driving test.

It's meant to challenge you and that is a good thing. But please remember, the one thing that will almost guarantee that you will pass is that you are SAFE.

Safe means that you have made decisions that will allow the smooth progress of your vehicle and that of others through any situation. That you have not placed anyone in danger or risked damaging another person's property. Every decision you make must be a safe one.

Thankyou for reading this book. I hope you have found it useful. If you have then please tell your friends. If you've not enjoyed it then please tell me.

Enjoy your driving.

For more help and advice, you can visit www.wyedrive.co.uk or follow WyeDrive on Facebook or Twitter.

USEFUL LINKS

The Driver and Vehicle Licensing Agency
https://www.gov.uk/government/organisations/driver-and-vehicle-licensing-agency

The Driving and Vehicle Standards Agency
https://www.gov.uk/government/organisations/driver-and-vehicle-standards-agency

The Highway Code
https://www.gov.uk/guidance/the-highway-code

RoSPA Advanced Drivers and Riders (RoADAR)
https://www.roadar.org.uk/

Institute of Advanced Motorists (IAM Roadsmart)
https://www.iamroadsmart.com/

Think Road Safety
https://www.think.gov.uk/

Book Your Theory Test
https://www.gov.uk/book-theory-test

Book Your Driving Test
https://www.gov.uk/book-driving-test

Become a Driving Instructor
https://www.gov.uk/become-a-driving-instructor

WyeDrive Driving School
https://www.wyedrive.co.uk/

Your Driving Details

My Driving Instructor is	
Driving Instructors Contact Details	
My first driving lesson date is	

Theory Test Date		Pass / Fail
Theory Test Date		Pass / Fail
Theory Test Date		Pass / Fail
Practical Test Date		Pass / Fail
Practical Test Date		Pass / Fail
Practical Test Date		Pass / Fail

Things to do:

Printed in Great Britain
by Amazon